Word Roots and Affixes Bingo Book

COMPLETE BINGO GAME IN A BOOK

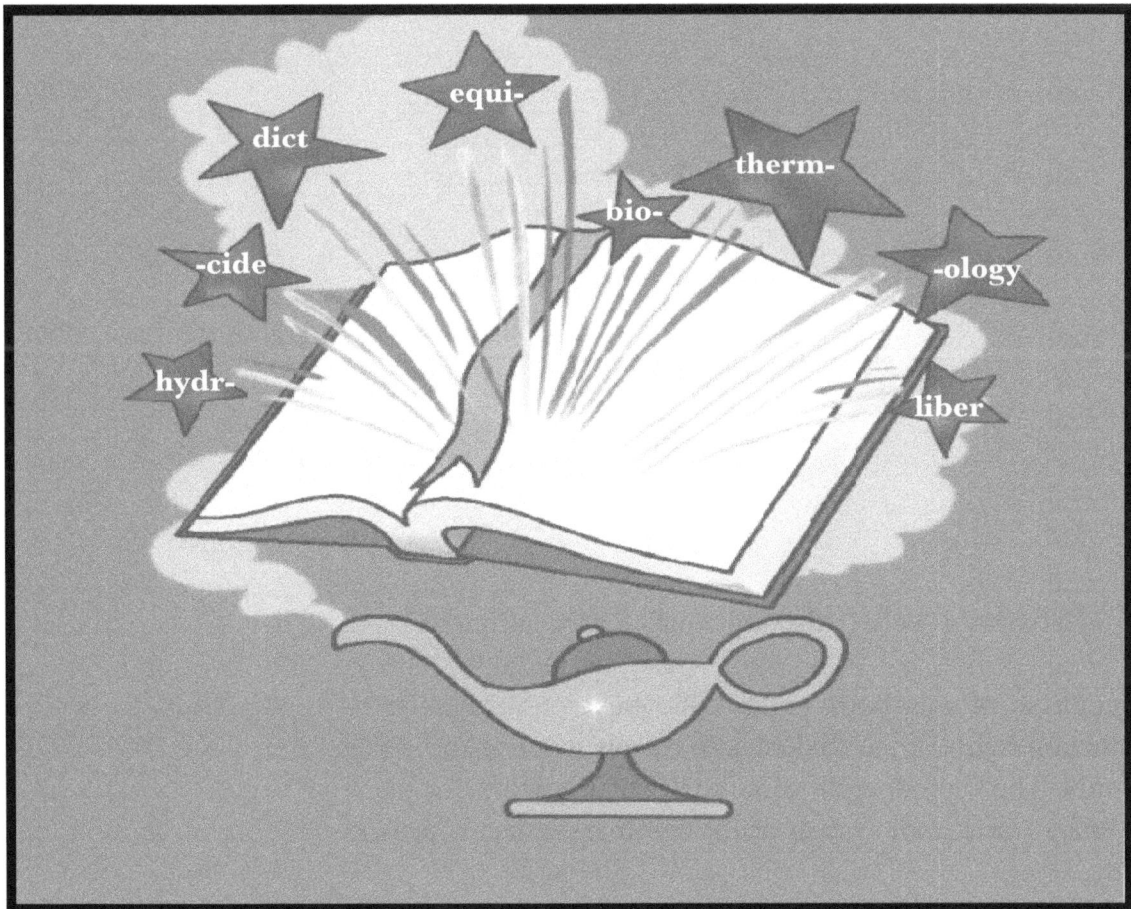

Written By Rebecca Stark

Educational Books 'n' Bingo

TITLE: Word Roots and Affixes Bingo
AUTHOR: Rebecca Stark

ISBN 978-0-87386-426-8

Educational Books 'n' Bingo

Printed in the U.S.A.

WORD ROOTS BINGO
Directions

INCLUDED:

List of Terms

Templates for Additional Terms and Clues

2 Clues per Term

30 Unique Bingo Cards

Markers

1. **Either cut apart the book or make copies of ALL the sheets. You might want to make an extra copy of the clue sheets to use for introduction and review. Keep the sheets in an envelope for easy reuse.**

2. Cut apart the call cards with terms and clues.

3. Pass out one bingo card per student. There are enough for a class of 30.

4. Pass out markers. You may cut apart the markers included in this book or use any other small items of your choice.

5. Decide whether or not you will require the entire card to be filled. Requiring the entire card to be filled provides a better review. However, if you have a short time to fill, you may prefer to have them do the just the border or some other format. Tell the class before you begin what is required.

6. There are 50 topics. Read the list before you begin. If there are any topics that have not been covered in class, you may want to read to the students the topic and clues before you begin.

7. There is a blank space in the middle of each card. You can instruct the students to use it as a free space or you can write in answers to cover topics not included. Of course, in this case you would create your own clues. (Templates provided.)

8. Shuffle the cards and place them in a pile. Two or three clues are provided for each topic. If you plan to play the game with the same group more than once, you might want to choose a different clue for each game. If not, you may choose to use more than one clue.

9. Be sure to keep the cards you have used for the present game in a separate pile. When a student calls, "Bingo," he or she will have to verify that the correct answers are on his or her card AND that the markers were placed in response to the proper questions. Pull out the cards that are on the student's card keeping them in the order they were used in the game. Read each clue as it was given and ask the student to identify the correct answer from his or her card.

10. If the student has the correct answers on the card AND has shown that they were marked in response to the *correct questions,* then that student is the winner and the game is over. If the student does not have the correct answers on the card OR he or she marked the answers in response to *the wrong questions,* then the game continues until there is a proper winner.

11. If you want to play again, reshuffle the cards and begin again.

Have Fun!

TERMS

astr	ter
auto	loc
belli	ogy / ology
bio	ly
breve	man
card	mar
chron	migra
cide	mit
corp	mort
cred	pac
dict	ped
dura	phon
equi	photo
er / or	port
fin	rupt
fix	scope
fort	spect
frag	tang
geo	therm
grad	tract
hydr	vac
il/ im / in / ir	ver
ject	viv
less	voc
liber	vol

Additional Terms

Choose as many additional terms as you would like and write them in the squares. Repeat each as desired.
Cut out the squares and randomly distribute them to the class.
Instruct the students to place their square on the center space of their card.

Word Roots and Affixes Bingo

Clues for Additional Terms

Write three clues for each of your additional terms.

_____ 1. 2. 3.	_____ 1. 2. 3.
_____ 1. 2. 3.	_____ 1. 2. 3.
_____ 1. 2. 3.	_____ 1. 2. 3.

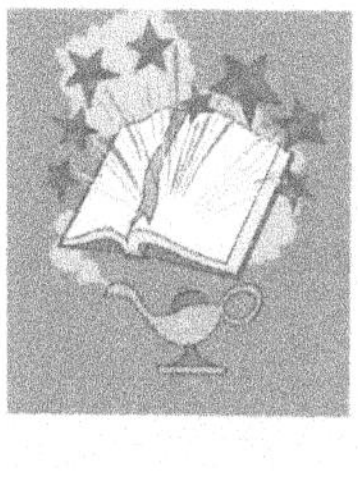
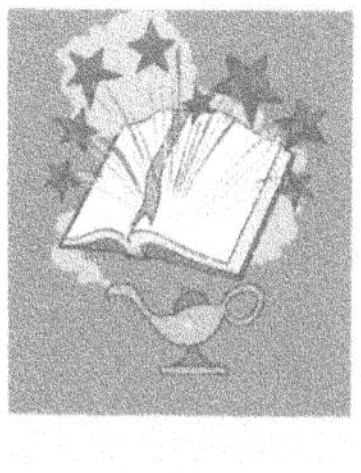
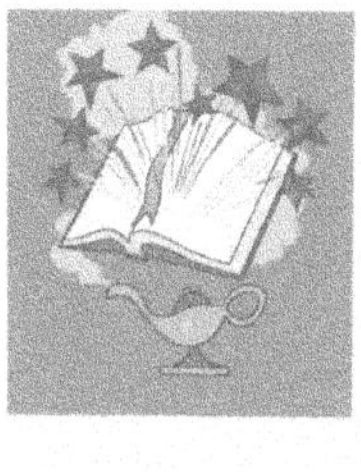
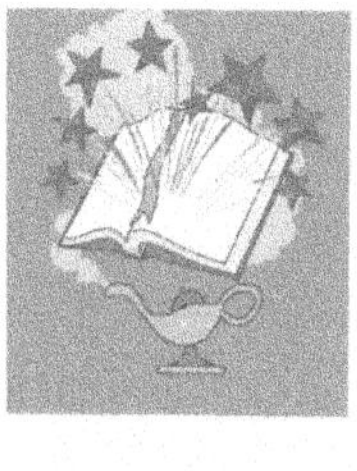
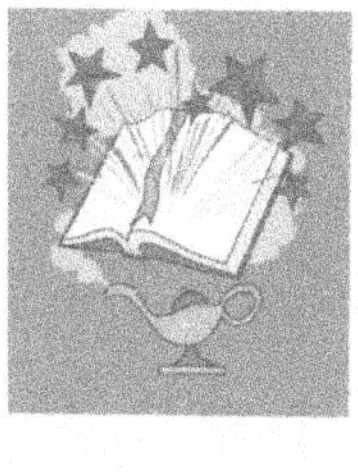
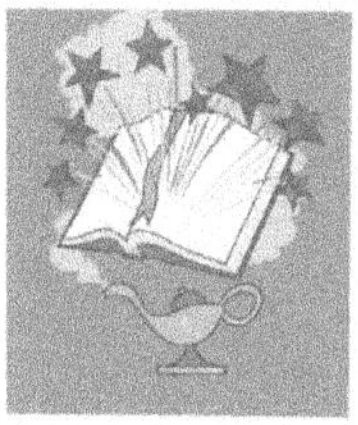
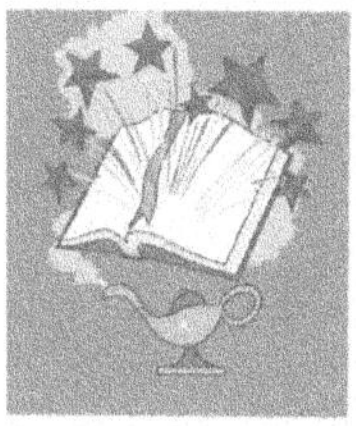
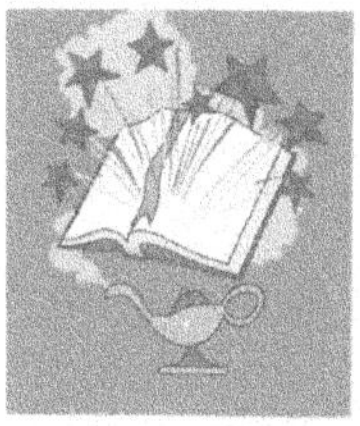
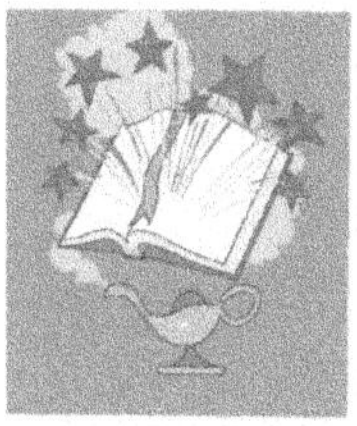
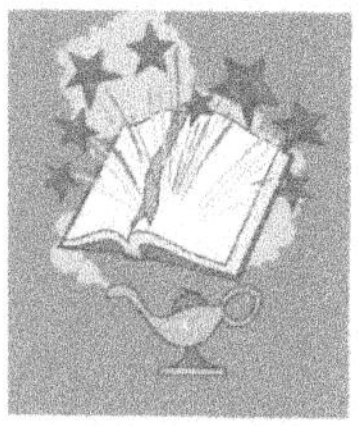
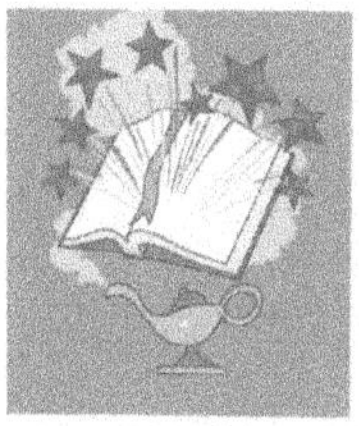
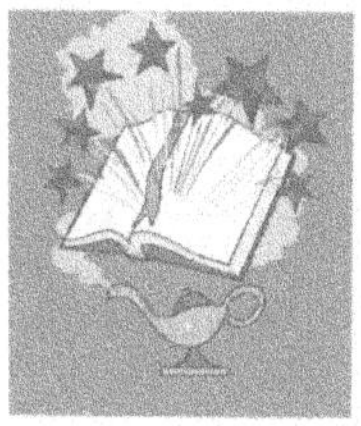
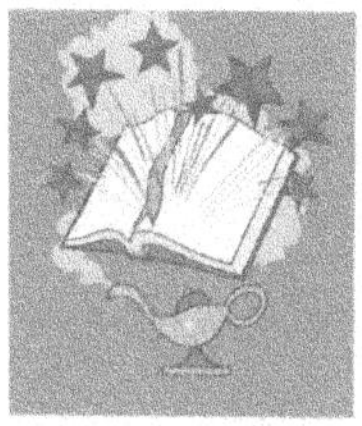
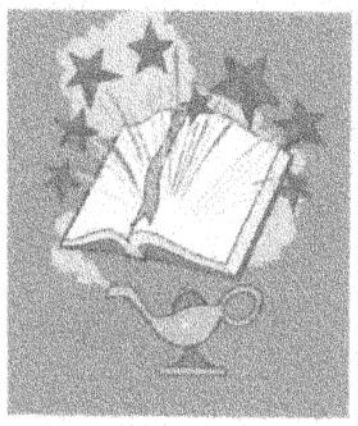
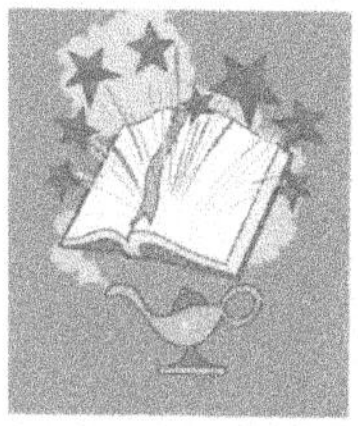
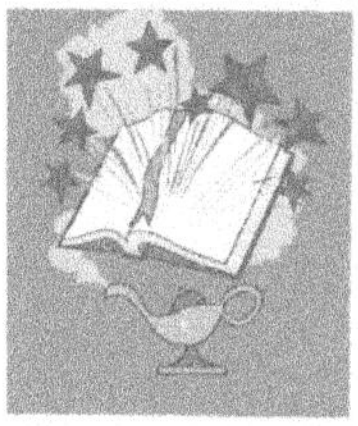
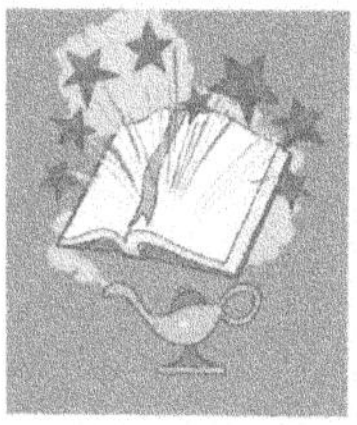
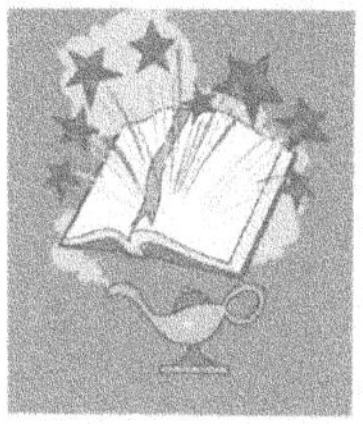
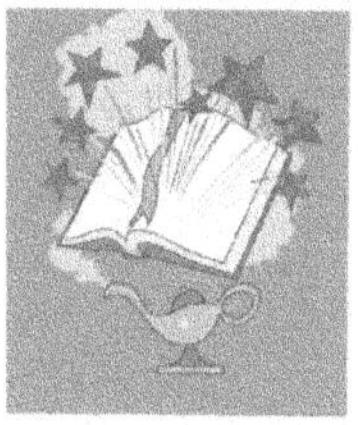
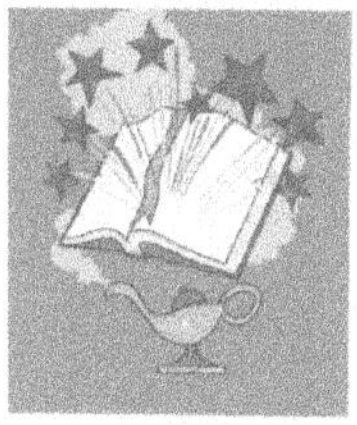
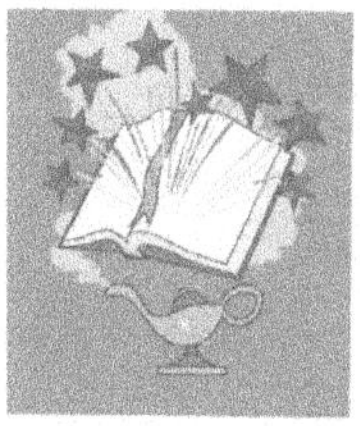
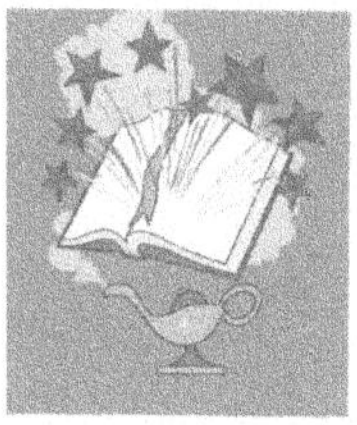
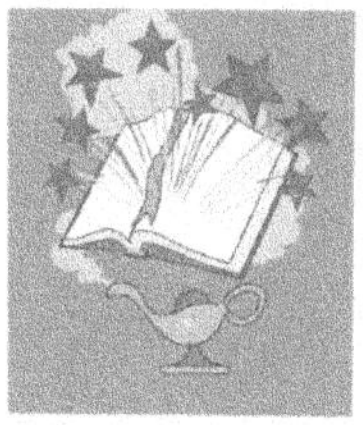
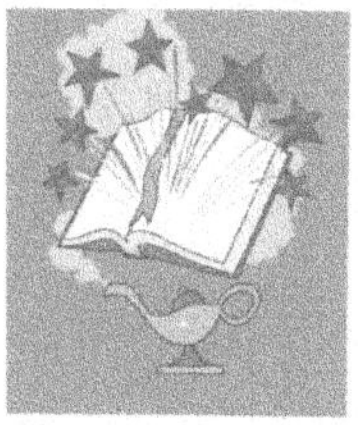
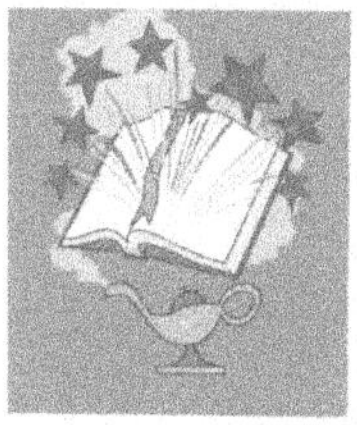
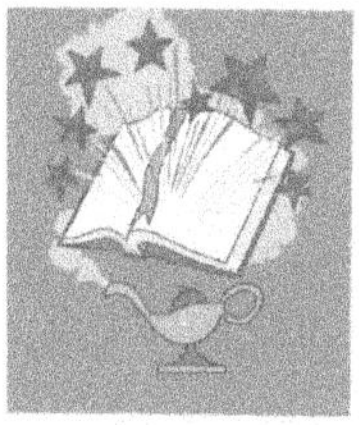
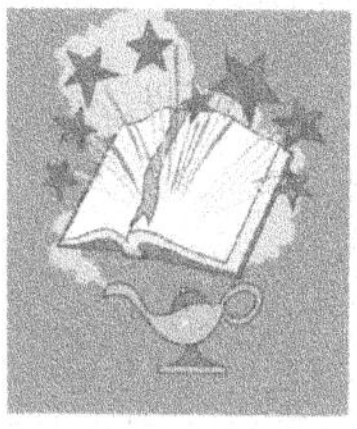
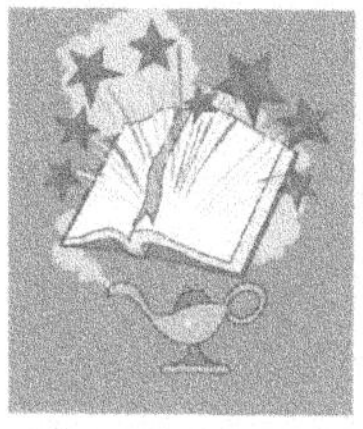
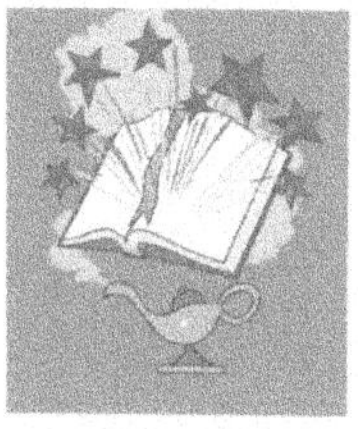
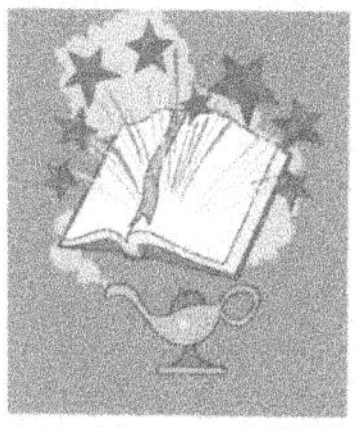
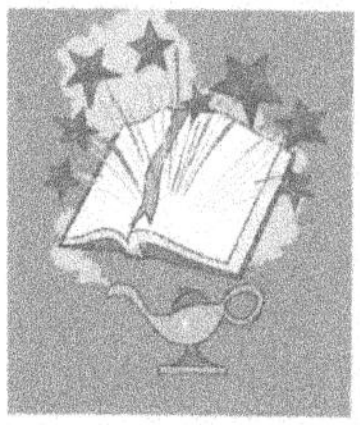
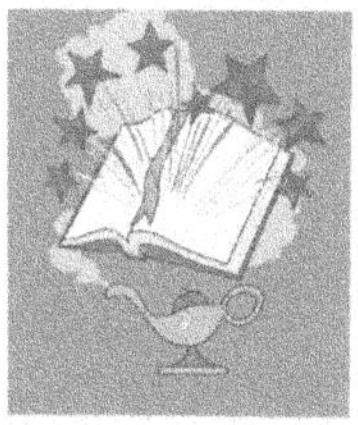
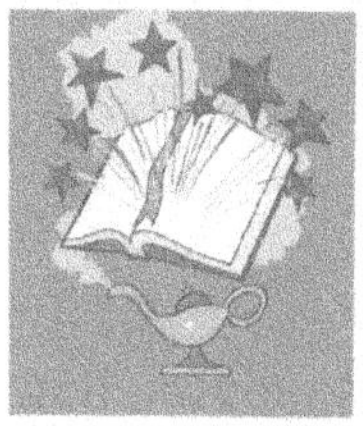
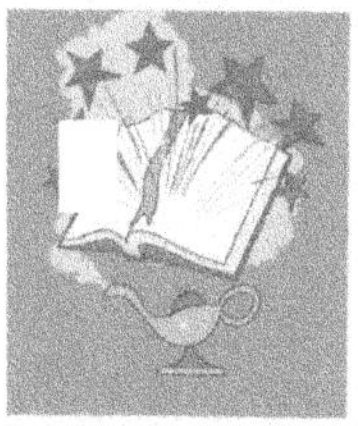
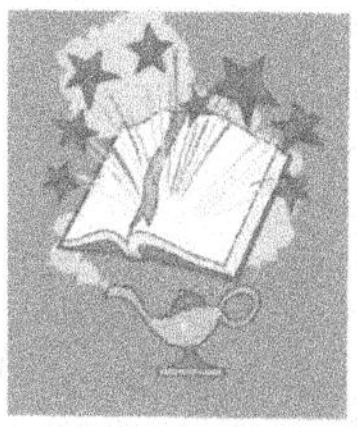

astr / astro	**auto**
1.This root means "star." 2. If you add the suffix -nomy, which means "a body of knowledge" to this root, you get a word meaning "the study of objects in outer space." 3. If you add the suffix -naut, which comes from a Greek word meaning "sailor," you get a word meaning "a person who travels into outer space."	1.This root means "self." 2. If you add the suffix -graph to this root, you get a word that means "a person's own signature." 3. If you add the suffix -matic to this root, you get a word that means "self-acting."
belli	**bio**
1. This root means "war." 2. The words belligerent and bellicose are based upon this root. 3. If you add the prefix re- and the suffix -on to this root,you get a word that means "defiance or resistance against authority."	1. This root means "life." 2. If you combine this root with the suffix -logy, you will get a word that means "the scientific study of life." 3. If you combine this root with the suffix -logist, you will get a word that means "someone who studies life."
brev	**card / cardi**
1. This root means "short." 2. It is the root of the word abbreviate, meaning "to reduce to a shorter form." 3. If you add the suffix -ity, which means "state or quality of," you get a word meaning "the quality of being brief" or "the shortness of time."	1. This root means "heart." 2. If you add the suffix -iac to this root, you get a word that means "having to do with the heart." 3. If you add the suffix -ology, to this root, you get a word that means "the study of the heart."
chron / chrono	**cide**
1. This root means "time." 2. If you combine this root with the word logical, you get a word meaning "arranged in order of time." 3. If you add the suffix -ic to this root, you get a word meaning "of long duration."	1. This suffix means "to kill." 2. If you add this suffix to homi-, you get a word that means "a person who kills another." 3. If you add this suffix to geno-. you get a word that means "the destruction of a group or race of people."
corp	**cred**
1. This root means "body." 2. If you add -oral to this root, you get a word which means "relating to the body." 3. If you add -ulent to this root, you get a word which means "having a large, bulky body."	1. This root means "believe." 2. If you add the suffix -ible, which means "capable of," you get a word that means "capable of being believed." 3. If you add the suffix -ible and the prefix in-, which means "not," you get a word that means "too improbable to be believed."

Word Roots and Affixes Bingo

dict 1. This root means "to say or speak." 2. If you add the prefix *pre-,* meaning "earlier" or "before," you get a word that means "to declare in advance." 3. If you add the prefix *ver-,* meaning "true," you get a noun that means "the decision of the jury."	**dur / dure** 1. This root means "hard or lasting." 2. If you add the prefix *-able,* you get a word that means "able to last a long time." 3. If you add the prefix *-en* to this root, you get a word that means "to undergo a hardship."
equi 1. This root means "equal." 2. It is the root for a word that means "the imaginary line that divides the northern and southern hemispheres." 3. If you combine this with *lateral,* meaning "relating to the side," you get an adjective that means "having all sides equal."	**er** or **or** 1. These suffix es mean "one who" or "that which." 2. If you add this suffix to the verb *play,* you get a noun meaning "one who plays." 3. If you add this suffix to the verb *act,* you get a noun meaning "one who acts."
fin 1. This root means "end." 2. If you add the suffix *-al* to this root, you will get a word that means "coming at the end." 3. If you add the suffix *-ale* to this root, you will get a noun that means "the closing part of a performance."	**fix** 1. This root means "to attach." 2. If you add the prefix *-pre,* you get a word that means "an affix attached to the beginning of a word." 3. If you add the prefix *-suf,* you get a word that means "an affix attached to the end of a word."
fort 1. This root means "strong." 2. If you add the suffix *-ress* to this root, you get a word meaning "a strong, secure place." 3. If you add the suffix *-ify* to this root, which means "to cause to become," you get a verb which means "to make strong."	**frag** 1. This root means "break." 2. If you add the suffix *-ment,* you get a word that means "a part broken off." 3. If you add the suffix *-ile,* you get a word that means "easily broken."
geo 1. This root means "earth." 2. If you add the suffix, *-logy,* you get a word that means "the study of the history of the earth." 3. If you add the suffix, *-graphy,* you get a word that means "the study of the features of the earth."	**grad** 1. This root means "step." 2. If you add the suffix *-ual* to this root, you get a word meaning "proceeding by steps or degrees." 3. If you add *-uate* to this root, you get a word meaning "to advance to a new level of achievement."

Word Roots and Affixes Bingo

hydr 1. This root means "water." 2. If you add the suffix -ate, you get a word that means "to cause to take up or combine with water." 3. If you add the suffix -ate and the prefix de-, you get a word that means "to remove water from."	**il / im / in / ir** 1. These prefixes mean "not." 2. If you add one of these prefixes to the word possible, you get a word meaning "not possible." 3. If you add one of these prefixes to the word regular, you get a word meaning "not regular."
ject 1. This root means "throw." 2. If you add the prefix -e, you get a word meaning "to throw out." 3. If you add the prefix inter-, you get a word meaning "to throw in between or among things."	**less** 1. This suffix means "lacking or without." 2. If you add this suffix to the word clue, you get a word meaning "having no clue." 3. If you add this suffix to the word worth, you get a word meaning "having no worth."
liber 1. This root means "free." 2. If you add the suffix -ty to this root, you get a word meaning "freedom." 3. If you add the suffix -ate to this root, you get a word meaning "to make free."	**liter** 1. This root means "letters." 2. If you add the suffix -al to this root, you get a word meaning "conforming to the primary meaning of a word." 3. A word that means "the repetition of initial consonant sounds in two or more neighboring words" has this as its root.
loc / loco 1. This root means "place." 2. If you add -motion to the end of this root, you get a word that means "the act or power of moving from place to place." 3. If you add the suffix -ate, you get a word that means "to determine the place of."	**logy / ology** 1. This suffix means "the study of." 2. If you add the prefix zo- to this root, you get a word that means "the branch of science dealing with the study of animals." 3. If you add the prefix myth- to this root, you get a word that means "the branch of knowledge dealing with myths."
ly 1. This suffix is used most often to change adjectives into adverbs. 2. If you add this suffix to soft, the result will be an adverb. 3. When this is at the end of a word, the word is usually, but not always, an adverb.	**man** 1. This root means "hand." 2. If you add the suffix -age to this root, you get a word meaning "to handle with some skill." 3. If you add -ual to this root, you get a word meaning "involving the hands."

mar 1. This root means "sea." 2. If you add the suffix *-ine* to this root, you get a word meaning "of or relating to the sea." 3. If you add *-ina* to this root, you get a word meaning "a dock or basin with moorings for pleasure boats."	**migr** 1. This root means "to move." 2. If you add the prefix *e-* and the suffix *-ate*, you get a word meaning "to leave one's country in order to live somewhere else." 3. If you add the prefix *im-* and the suffix *-ate*, you get a word meaning "to to come into a country of which one is not a native in order to live there."
mit 1. This root means "to send." 2. If you add the prefix *sub-* to this root, you get a word meaning "to present for consideration." 3. If you add the prefix *trans-* to this root, you get a word meaning "to send or convey from one person or place to another."	**mort** 1. This root means "death." 2. If you add the suffix *-al* to this word, you get a word meaning "subject to death." 3. If you add the suffix *-al* and the prefix *im-* to this word, you get a word meaning "exempt from death."
pac 1. This root means "peace." 2. If you add the suffix *-ify,* which means "to make or to become," to this root, you get a word meaning "to ease the anger." 3. If you add *-ifist* to this root, you get a word meaning "opposed to conflict, especially war."	**ped** 1. This root means "foot." 2. If you add the suffix *-al* to this root, you get a word meaning "a lever pressed by the foot." 3. If you add *-estrian* to this root, you get a word meaning "one who goes by foot."
phon 1. This root means "sound." 2. If you add the suffix *-eme* to this root, you get a word meaning "the smallest unit of sound that can convey distinction in meaning." 3. If you add the prefix *sym-* and the suffix *-y* to this root, you get a word meaning "a musical piece for a large orchestra."	**photo** 1. This root means "light." 2. If you add the suffix *-graphy* to this root, you get a word meaning "a process that uses light to produce images." 3. If someone is ___ sensitive, that person is sensitive to light.
port 1. This root means "carry." 2. If you add the prefix *trans-* to this root, you get a word meaning "to carry or transfer from one place to another." If you add the prefix *ex-* to this root, you get a word meaning "to sell or transfer to another place." 3. If you add the prefix *sup-* to this root, you get a word meaning "to bear the weight of." Word Roots and Affixes Bingo	**rupt** 1. This root means "break." 2. If you add the suffix *-ure* to this root, you get a word meaning "the process or state of being broken open." 3. If you add the prefix *inter-* to this root, you get a word meaning "to break the continuity of." © **Barbara M Peller**

scope 1. This root means "to see or watch." 2. If you add the prefix *tele-* to this root, you get a word meaning "an instrument used in astronomy to view distant objects." 3. If you add the prefix *micro-* to this root, you get a word meaning "an instrument that magnifies small objects so that we can see them in more detail."	**tang** 1. This root means "touch." 2. If you add the suffix *-ible* to this root, you get a word meaning "discernible to the touch." 3. If you add the suffix *-ible* and the prefix *in-*, you get a word meaning "not discernible to the touch."
spect 1. This root means "to look at." 2. If you add the suffix *-acles* to this root, you get a word meaning "eyeglasses." 3. If you add *-ator* to this root, you get a word meaning "one who looks on or watches."	**therm** 1. This root means "heat." 2. If you add the suffix *-os* to this root, you get a word meaning "a container designed to keep liquids hot or cold." 3. If you add the suffix *-al* to this root, you get a word meaning "related to or caused by heat."
tract 1. This root means "to draw or pull." 2. If you add the suffix *-or* to this root, you get a word meaning "a machine used to draw or pull farm equipment." 3. If you add the prefix *at-* to this root, you get a word meaning "to pull toward oneself or itself."	**vac** 1. This root means "empty." 2. If you add the suffix *-ate* to this root, you get a word that means "to make empty of occupants." 3. If you add the suffix *-ant* to this root, you get a word that means "not occupied or lived in."
ver 1. This root means "truth." 2. If you add the suffix *-ify* to this root, you get a word that means "to confirm or establish the truth." 3. If you add the suffix *-dict* to this root, you get a word that means "the finding of a jury."	**viv / vive** 1. This root means "alive." 2. If you add the prefix *re-* to this root, you get a word that means "to restore life." 3. If you add the prefix *sur-* to this root, you get a word that means "to live on or to remain alive."
voc 1. This root means "call." 2. If you add the prefix *-al* to this root, you get a word that means "relating to the voice." 3. If you add the prefix *ad-* and the suffix *-ate,* you get a word that means "one who pleads the cause of another."	**vol** 1. This root means "will." 2. If you add the prefix *male-* and the suffix *-ent,* you get a word that means "marked by vicious ill will." 3. If you add the prefix *bene-* and the suffix *-ent,* you get a word that means "marked by good will."

Word Roots and Affixes Bingo

Word Roots and Affixes Bingo

photo	astr	belli	geo	breve
fin	auto	viv	man	scope
ver	ter		pac	voc
vac	rupt	tract	ly	less
mort	il / im / in / ir	fort	tang	liber

© **Barbara M Peller**

Word Roots and Affixes Bingo

vac	ver	less	port	ogy / ology
migra	fix	cide	rupt	mit
cred	il / im / in / ir		ject	tract
ped	phon	ter	vol	breve
scope	viv	fort	fin	tang

Word Roots and Affixes Bingo

il / im / in / ir	tract	fix	ly	ver
migra	auto	corp	astr	hydr
rupt	viv		mit	bio
ter	cred	mort	ped	less
tang	dict	fort	vol	ogy / ology

Word Roots and Affixes Bingo

ter	mit	belli	dict	ogy / ology
mar	chron	astr	port	ver
pac	ped		liber	geo
tract	ter	viv	fort	cide
dura	scope	card	tang	voc

© Barbara M Peller

Word Roots and Affixes Bingo

scope	breve	rupt	cide	dict
mar	tract	corp	ject	auto
belli	voc		man	grad
liber	ogy / ology	photo	vol	equi
fix	fort	ver	ter	pac

Word Roots and Affixes Bingo

bio	mit	fix	ogy / ology	voc
ly	rupt	equi	astr	ver
port	dura		chron	ject
fort	mort	vol	card	belli
migra	cide	photo	pac	er / or

Word Roots and Affixes Bingo

photo	voc	grad	tract	fix
migra	ogy / ology	il / im / in / ir	auto	mar
less	geo		ject	chron
ter	ped	corp	vac	cred
fort	dict	vol	card	bio

Word Roots and Affixes Bingo

pac	mit	frag	ly	chron
mar	belli	port	voc	cide
er / or	dict		ogy / ology	breve
tang	ter	vac	dura	ped
viv	fort	card	rupt	migra

Word Roots and Affixes Bingo

ject	fix	il / im / in / ir	er / or	dict
dura	ogy / ology	pac	rupt	mit
hydr	photo		auto	frag
equi	breve	mort	man	grad
ped	vol	corp	vac	liber

Word Roots and Affixes Bingo

vac	ly	chron	port	er / or
voc	cide	astr	auto	ogy / ology
dict	mit		geo	cred
mort	liber	equi	vol	hydr
corp	migra	fix	scope	pac

© Barbara M Peller

Word Roots and Affixes Bingo

bio	mit	rupt	equi	migra
frag	hydr	man	ject	astr
mar	ogy / ology		fin	il / im / in / ir
corp	ver	vol	dict	vac
dura	fort	photo	card	fix

Word Roots and Affixes Bingo

fix	breve	hydr	ly	ject
il / im / in / ir	migra	belli	card	auto
photo	grad		voc	port
fort	ped	ogy / ology	vac	mar
mit	frag	dict	dura	cide

Word Roots and Affixes Bingo

equi	breve	bio	hydr	voc
belli	frag	ogy / ology	ject	cred
ly	cide		il / im / in / ir	grad
pac	vol	chron	dict	vac
fort	liber	card	photo	man

Word Roots and Affixes Bingo

fin	ogy / ology	rupt	ject	dura
cide	photo	hydr	auto	mit
equi	geo		less	corp
liber	vol	dict	chron	bio
fort	port	cred	migra	pac

Word Roots and Affixes Bingo

man	ject	rupt	fix	ly
bio	fin	astr	belli	dura
voc	photo		ver	mit
fort	hydr	frag	vol	equi
migra	ped	card	er / or	il / im / in / ir

Word Roots and Affixes Bingo

chron	hydr	frag	er / or	phon
port	cred	grad	mar	geo
equi	breve		voc	il / im / in / ir
ter	cide	fort	man	vac
dura	therm	card	ped	mit

Word Roots and Affixes Bingo

corp	spect	loc	hydr	fin
man	dura	vol	geo	grad
ject	pac		therm	frag
liber	migra	vac	rupt	cred
mort	equi	fix	ly	breve

Word Roots and Affixes Bingo

er / or	dict	cide	equi	port
mit	corp	mort	voc	dura
ject	cred		loc	belli
breve	astr	vol	vac	less
therm	hydr	rupt	spect	bio

© Barbara M Peller

Word Roots and Affixes Bingo

voc	bio	hydr	frag	vac
man	ly	mit	fix	geo
spect	dict		auto	ver
less	therm	mort	ped	loc
belli	phon	migra	pac	card

© Barbara M Peller

Word Roots and Affixes Bingo

fin	spect	ly	hydr	card
cide	il / im / in / ir	mar	mort	port
breve	grad		ter	astr
scope	viv	tang	ped	therm
tract	pac	phon	vac	loc

© Barbara M Peller

Word Roots and Affixes Bingo

man	bio	mar	hydr	scope
breve	loc	chron	frag	photo
cred	migra		spect	rupt
mort	fix	therm	liber	pac
ter	phon	card	corp	ped

Word Roots and Affixes Bingo

er / or	less	loc	belli	equi
port	ly	ver	frag	auto
cide	geo		photo	grad
therm	liber	ped	astr	mar
phon	corp	spect	cred	less

Word Roots and Affixes Bingo

chron	spect	fix	belli	card
bio	fin	migra	man	astr
less	equi		tang	photo
cred	phon	therm	corp	ped
scope	viv	pac	mort	loc

Word Roots and Affixes Bingo

chron	pac	fin	spect	frag
loc	card	mar	port	photo
grad	er / or		equi	cred
scope	tang	therm	corp	breve
tract	ter	phon	ly	viv

Word Roots and Affixes Bingo

ter	mar	spect	rupt	loc
astr	breve	man	chron	auto
liber	frag		tang	therm
ver	scope	viv	phon	geo
card	fin	cide	dura	tract

Word Roots and Affixes Bingo

loc	spect	less	port	er / or
mort	ly	frag	fin	chron
liber	tang		geo	ter
corp	belli	scope	phon	therm
grad	dura	rupt	viv	tract

Word Roots and Affixes Bingo

less	cide	spect	fin	il / im / in / ir
scope	tang	man	therm	auto
vol	viv		phon	ter
er / or	bio	mar	tract	astr
dura	geo	loc	ver	grad

Word Roots and Affixes Bingo

less	fin	ver	spect	chron
il / im / in / ir	loc	tang	port	geo
viv	cred		grad	mort
vac	er / or	migra	phon	therm
belli	ject	dura	tract	scope

Word Roots and Affixes Bingo

loc	fin	er / or	man	ject
ped	mort	mar	grad	ver
liber	tang		auto	spect
il / im / in / ir	scope	ogy / ology	phon	therm
chron	frag	tract	bio	viv

Word Roots and Affixes Bingo

dict	spect	port	ject	therm
astr	fin	fix	geo	auto
liber	equi		grad	mar
tract	bio	belli	phon	tang
scope	voc	viv	loc	ver